AF604298

For Tanya, who helps in so many beautiful ways ~ DB

For Mrs McLaughlin ~ HJT

'How far that little candle
throws his beams!
So shines a good deed
in a weary world.'

– WILLIAM SHAKESPEARE

A Lothian Children's Book

Published in Australia and New Zealand in 2025
by Hachette Australia
Gadigal Country, Level 17, 207 Kent Street, Sydney NSW 2000
www.hachettechildrens.com.au

Hachette Australia acknowledges and pays our respects to the past, present and future Traditional Owners and Custodians of Country throughout Australia and recognises the continuation of cultural, spiritual and educational practices of Aboriginal and Torres Strait Islander peoples. Our head office is located on the lands of the Gadigal people of the Eora Nation.

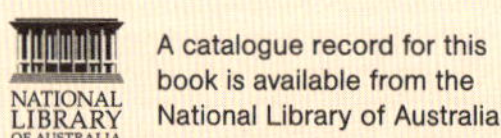
A catalogue record for this book is available from the National Library of Australia

ISBN: 978 0 7344 2365 8 (hardback)

Designed by Kirby Armstrong
Colour reproduction by Splitting Image
Printed in China by Toppan Leefung Printing Limited

HOW TO HELP

when you really want to help

DAVINA BELL
+ HILARY JEAN TAPPER

LOTHIAN Children's Books

A tissue for a tear.

A cloth to clean.

Somewhere to stay.

Something to snuggle.

Baking.

Making.

Your voice.

Your ears.

Your heart.

Open arms.

Mending fingers.

A friendly face.

A soft place to land.

LOST
LOST
LOST
Spreading the word.

A letterbox treat.

Stopping by.

Giving away.

Checking in.

showing how.

Showing up.

Cleaning up.

Standing up!

Or standing aside.

Gathering together.

Staying till the end.

Being there
again tomorrow.

Whenever you help,

however you do,

the person you're helping is actually...

you.